The Virtuous Business Woman: Inspired by
Proverbs 31

Second Edition

Tammie T. Polk

ISBN-10: **1541282760**

ISBN-13: **978-1541282766**

DEDICATION

This second edition is still for…

All the women who see the need to be virtuous.

All the women who endeavor to be virtuous.

All the women who understand what virtue is.

The women who want to be virtuous in every area

of their lives.

YOU!

**Here's to the Virtuous Woman…again. May we
be them, know them, and raise them!**

CONTENTS

Introduction

The thoughts behind this book came shortly after I published *From One King's Daughter to Another.* I wanted to get to work on something else. Proverbs 31 is one of my favorite passages of scripture and I wanted to do something with it. First, I decided to write another book for girls using Proverbs 31 as the base, which is still in the works. Then it hit me—applying Proverbs 31 to the business world! I grabbed my Bible and wrote Proverbs 31:10-31 out, prayed over it, and watched it unfold before my eyes.

Each chapter of this book begins with one verse from this classic passage, with the exception of one that has two. My intention with The Virtuous Business Woman is for you to see that there is more to this passage than just marriage and family. The Word of God is truly inexhaustible!

Although it is written from the entrepreneur's point of view, it's really for any woman in a managerial or supervisory position. And, even though it is written to women, it can also apply to men in a lot of areas, so don't be afraid to share this book with a man that you know! I've considered revamping this for a man, which I may very well do.

The worksheets are there to help you to process the reading. The verse is there to keep you from having to flip back through and find it. The main points are there to help remind you of what was talked about in the reading. The TVBW Action Plan serves as sort of a "What do I do next" guide in response to what you read and what your reflections are on the reading. The questions are there to make you think—and hard. These questions are your reality check!

Before you start your journey, pray! This is going to be quite the eye-opening experience. I saw that as I wrote. It is my hope that you understand what is written here and are able to apply it wherever you may find yourself at this point. God Bless!

But, before you go, I want you to know why I rereleased the book, so in this case ONLY, it's okay to skip to the end!

1 PURPOSE TO BE VIRTUOUS

Proverbs 31:10- "Who can find a virtuous woman? For her price is far above rubies."

Take a moment and think about the word "virtue." What exactly is virtue anyway? Many have their own definition for this word. I prefer the one that my pastor uses. He says that virtue is having moral excellence, meaning that you make a conscious decision to do what is right and then graduate to doing what is best. This is exactly what a virtuous woman endeavors to do.

A virtuous business woman has, exhibits, and maintains both personal and professional integrity. Known as a woman of her word, she is nowhere near perfect, but people should be speaking highly of her. Words such unfair, uncaring, uncooperative, untrustworthy, should not describe her!

A virtuous business woman is truthful, fair, and firm in all business dealings. A virtuous business woman is not one that cheats people, takes advantage of them, overcharges them, or undercuts them. She should not misuse nor mistreat anyone she is in business with. It not only creates problems for her business, but it also brings reproach on the name of Christ. How many times have you heard someone say something like this: "He/she claims to be a Christian and they have done this to me or that to me." A virtuous business woman maintains a consistent testimony in all that she says and does.

A virtuous business woman does what is right, even if it means losing clients, money, or business relationships. Now, this is a hard pill to swallow. In today's business world, we look for those important business connections that will help us get to the next level. Sometimes we will lay our convictions aside for the sake of the business, which can lead to trouble. This has been my experience. Last year, a business relationship ended very badly. I knew what this person was about, but I focused on national recognition from being associated with her and I did not take the stand that I needed to. When the time came to deal with the situation, I was in tears because I did not want to sever the relationship because I knew that there was not going to be another opportunity like that one. This person blasted me to the hilt and, to be honest, I deserved every bit of it. Had I taken the stand that a virtuous business woman should have, things might have gone differently.

A virtuous business woman is guided by the principles of God's Word, even in business. If I tried to lay out every verse in the Bible that shows how we are to run our businesses as virtuous business women, this book would be as long as a dictionary! However, I will mention one, 2 Corinthians 6:14- "Be ye not unequally yoked together with unbelievers: for what fellowship hath righteousness with unrighteousness? and what communion hath light with darkness?" Most people see that verse and think about marriage, but the same rules apply in the business world.

A virtuous business woman is careful with who she links up with. Not every relationship that looks good to your business may be for your business. Do your research on people that want to link up with you. Find out who their customer base really is. Find out what causes they support. Find out to whom they donate money. Talk to other business owners who may have dealt with them in the past. See how the community around them feels about their business. How does their business concept line up with the Bible? Yes, it might seem like overkill, but knowledge is power for a reason. You just might be dodging a huge bullet.

A virtuous business woman uses discernment and good judgment. This goes along with our last point. Always pray and seek God's answers before pursuing anything in your business. Ask Him to help you to weed out and see through those who may both openly and secretly seek to destroy your business. Ask Him to help you to not fall for prey to their devices! There are so many business people out there today that look to take out their competition in any way possible. They may seem as though they come in peace, but their true intent is to tear your business into pieces! I am reminded of Solomon's wish when God asked him what he wanted Him to do for him. Look at I Kings 3:9- "Give therefore thy servant an understanding heart to judge thy people, that I may discern between good and bad: for who is able to judge this thy so great a people?" He did not ask for long life, riches, or anything like that—he asked for a discerning heart and wisdom so that he could lead Israel in the right way. We should be just like Solomon! Think about that for a moment.

A virtuous business woman knows her value. Everyone today seems to be looking for a handout, discount or something for little or nothing! A virtuous business woman understands her price and stands by it. She does not lower her prices to appease people, but shows how and why she is worth the price she gives. It is okay to have baby prices in the beginning, but do not shy away from the grown woman prices that you need to have to keep your business going. I had baby prices when I started out and many people were shocked at my prices. They thought I offered way too much for way too little of a price. I was surprised myself when I started using my grown woman rate and found that people actually understood why! I felt like I was moving in the right direction!

A virtuous business woman prices her services fairly, but competitively. Yes, this could have gone with the last point, but I decided to bring it to its own space for a reason. Coming up with a service outline and pricing structure are two of the hardest thing any business person does. I know that first hand. When I was coming up with mine, I spent hours looking at my competitors' websites and talking directly to them. I printed out everything I could, looked at what I knew I could offer as well, came up with a basic pricing structure, and then refined it. It was not an easy process, but it was something that I needed to go through. Why?

Recently, I had a client to bring up to me that one of my competitors charged half of what I did for the same services. I smiled as I listened to her compare our services. Once she was done, I asked her to look at one very important detail—the length of time. She got very quiet. What I was charging for a year round support package, meaning that she would receive services from me for nine to twelve months, this competitor was charging for three hours of her time. Anything over those three hours had additional fees: $20 for a phone call, $5 for email communication, etc. I was not charging her that way, though I previously had a similar pricing structure. Did I lock her? Yes, I did! And it is all because I stuck to my guns and showed her why and how I was the better choice.

A virtuous business woman does not undervalue herself or diminish her value. This may sound like the last few paragraphs, but it is different. How? It is because value means more than money. A virtuous business woman does not stoop to unfair and unethical business practices. Has anyone ever told you that you knew better than to do something or get involved with someone? They told you what you were worth more than that. They told you that you and your business are more valuable than that. And, now you have to spend time redeeming yourself and your company's reputation, which could take a very long time. You do not have time for that.

A virtuous business woman knows what she can and cannot do and does not misrepresent herself and/or her limitations. One of the worst things anyone in business can do is to say that they can do something that they know they cannot do! Do not do that to yourself! If someone asks you to do something that you cannot do or do not offer, offer to help them find someone that they can go to in order to get that done. In the meantime, you might want to learn how to do it for the next person that comes around. Once you are proficient at whatever it is, you can offer those services to the same client if they are unsatisfied with the person that they went to after speaking to you. It is better to be honest about it upfront than to lie and lose a lot more than you thought you would have!

Lastly, a virtuous business woman realizes that she has something rare and precious to offer, even in the wake of competition. You are unique. You are different. You are special. You can do something that the others cannot do at all or cannot do as well as you can. You have gifts and talents from God that are specifically designed for you to do what you are doing. You have taken the time to hone and perfect those skills. You have something that no one else has, no matter how similar you may be to them. That is not necessarily overconfidence! It could very well be the truth!

This first verse of The Virtuous Woman passage is chock full of things to think about and process. What I want you to do now is to look at the worksheet that I have prepared to go with this verse. Pray before answering any of the questions. Be honest with yourself. This, Ladies, is the first step to becoming a Virtuous Business Woman!

2 YOUR HUSBAND'S P LACE

Proverbs 31:11, 12—"The heart of her husband doth safely trust in her, so that he shall have no need of spoil. She will do him good and not evil all the days of her life."

I combined these two verses for a reason. A virtuous business woman honors her husband—if she has one—even in business! First and foremost, a virtuous business woman is faithful to her husband! She knows how to deal with men and keep it professional. There is no talk of her being or acting in an inappropriate manner with any man with whom she comes into contact with inside or outside of the business environment.. She should not do anything to undermine her marriage for the sake of her business, either! If she thinks that she would hurt her husband by doing what another man is asking her to do in return for what she needs for her business, she is not going to do it! She finds a better way to get what she needs because no other man or business relationship is worth the one that she has with her husband!

Her husband should know, feel, and understand her business, the vision for it, and the vision behind it, even if she feels as though he may not fully understand it. I am a married business woman and my husband is a behind the scenes type of guy, but he keeps me on the ground. I am eternally grateful for that. Even though he may not know all of the ins and outs of my business, there are some things that I know that he can help me with and I keep him informed!

He understands that her business exists to help support him and their home. This is a BIG one! Despite the successes you are experiencing in your business, he should never feel like his profession is second to yours. I have run across so many who feel that because own their own business, make more, or even have a more quality clientele, that they are better than their husband and what he is doing. No husband should ever feel completely left out! Yes, he may not speak to your cause in the way you may want him to, but he is trying!

I asked my husband if he would quit his job and come over into my business with me when I started to become busier and more successful. His response? He said that he would feel like he, as a man, was not contributing in the way a man should. He wanted to keep his hands on something and support his family in case something happened. While I was a little irritated about that, I had to step outside of myself and realize what he was saying. He was not trying to belittle or demean what I was doing. He was not trying to say that I would not need his help, nor was he saying he would not help me. However, like most women, those thoughts were the first to come to mind. He knows that my business is meant to compliment what he is doing and to help sustain the household, not to overrun and overrule it. That is hard for some to grasp a hold of, but it will keep down the conflict in your home. Let me expound on that point.

He knows that her business exists to compliment and not to compete with what he is doing nor undermine it. If your business makes more money than his, do not rub it in! Do not point it out…matter of fact, do not even mention it if he does not ask! A man wants to know that he's doing all that he can to maintain his household and wants to feel that he can carry the load, but may need your help from time to time. Do not get agitated if he wants to keep monies together and not split up. He may ask you to help your home out with money from the business. Something may happen and you have to step in financially. And, more importantly, should you have to use your business to save your home, NEVER THROW THAT IN HIS FACE! I do not care how bad it gets! He needs to know that you support him. He needs to know that he can count on you…which brings me to the next point.

He should feel that her business does not exist out of malice, envy, and ill will toward him. In other words, do not just up and start something because you are mad at him. Do not start a business because you are jealous of the attention and accolades he gets in his work. Do not start a business to prove a point—that is a two-edged sword. While you may very well accomplish the success and the monetary goals that you set, something is going to happen that is going to make you see why you should not have done things the way you did. Now, I am not saying that you should sit around and do nothing while things crumble around you. I am saying that you can do it with the right heart attitude and with better intentions. He should see you as trying to help him…please understand how important that is.

He should know that any success she achieves is not going to be thrown in his face and used against him. Did we just talk about this? Yes, we did a little bit, but I wanted to say more. At one time in my life, I found myself saying that I had to go back to work because what my husband was doing was not enough. I had to do something because it had gotten hard for us. I got up every day with that on my heart and, yes, I even allowed the words to come out of my mouth. I was making more money than he was at the time and I was able to take care of all the things that he could not at that point. However, ladies, I was so stressed out in it because I carried those thoughts with me every single day. Even when things got better, I still carried those thoughts with me. And, if we had an argument, I would bring it up only to hear him say that he was trying. Tears would fill my eyes because I knew it was true. I am so glad that we have moved beyond those days.

He should not feel like he is not excluded from the business and can help. Women do not realize this one thing until they have paid someone else to do it! Think about what your husband can do and see if it can be useful in your business. If he is good to bounce ideas off of, talk to him about what you are thinking of doing. He may be able to provide a different perspective that you might not have thought about. If he is good at organizing and putting things together, let him help you with your next workshop conference, or event. If he has good computer skills, let him help you with your website, presentations, and other things you may need. Honey, use your husband! I do. If I think for one minute that he can help me, I am asking him to do it. In fact, he looked over the outline for this very book! Do not leave him out.

He should know that her business is not meant to replace his. Remember the example I gave earlier? I am going to expound on that a little more.

You see, when I asked my husband that question, I had the best intentions. His job is a stressful one and I know that he is looking for a change, but I had to also understand that my business may not be that change. He may have something else that he wants to do. He may have a secret professional goal that I might not know about. As much as you may want to have him, it may not be the road that he wants to take. Yes, it may be frustrating; however, you have to realize that the gifts and talents that God gave him may not be suited for your business.

I understand that many of you, like me, started your businesses to help your husband. I understand that you want to alleviate some of the pressure and the stress that he is under. I understand that you want to shoulder some of the weight that is sitting on him. What I do not want you to do is to try to force him to leave what he is doing to come on board with you. While it may be a good idea right then, it may not be the right time! I had to realize that with my husband as well.

Honoring our husbands in our businesses is not always an easy thing to do, but it is the right thing to do. Your husband should never feel as though he is less of a man because of what you are doing and you should not treat him that way. He should not have to find ways to feel fulfilled and needed because you are so set on your business succeeding. Nevertheless, that is another story for another chapter.

Look at the worksheet for this verse. Think about your husband. Do you need to talk through and work some things out? If so, what are they? If you know what they are, are you willing to get it right? Pray about it and move forward when you are ready to do so.

3 BE SEEN, HEARD, AND FELT

Proverbs 31:13—"She seeketh wool, and flax, and worketh willingly with her hands."

A virtuous business woman educates herself! She takes the necessary steps to ensure professional growth for herself and growth for her business. It is beyond imperative that you stay on top of things in your realm of business. Getting caught off guard can lead to your business virtually vanishing from sight. What do I mean? Let us talk about it a while.

A virtuous business woman keeps up with trends that relate to her business. That means you are paying attention to what is going on. You know what works and what does not. You are trying new approaches that may help propel your business to the next level. You are constantly reading relevant periodicals and blogs so that you can stay up on what the needs are in your world. You try new apps and other software that is meant to enhance your business. You check out any new competition. It is all about staying relevant while maintain a God-honoring business!

A virtuous business woman actively advocates for and advertises her business. Do not be the best-kept secret in town! Let people know that you are out there. Let people know that you exist. Let people know what you have to offer. Let people know what makes you different. If you do not put yourself out there, you will not be out there. I found that out the hard way! I thought that my website and social media posts would do the work for me. No, ma'am! I had to start going to community events and vendor shows. I had to get out, hang flyers, and leave business cards in places where I knew I could help. I joined groups on social media that would help me get my name out in the way that

I wanted it to. I networked! Do not let your opportunities pass you by!

A virtuous business woman attends networking meetings, conferences, and workshops that enhance her professional skills and business offerings. I remember when I went to my first vendor sale. It was a homeschool used curriculum sale. I had some things that I needed to get rid of, but I gained more than money that day. I gained connections. Weird? Not really. Why? It is because I knew where the next sale was, who to contact, and what I could and could not do before I left that sale. I started to meet people who were interested in what I do. I was asked to speak to parent groups. I had guidance counselors at schools calling and asking me to speak to parents. Before I knew it, my husband pointed out something very important to me. He looked at me one day as I was preparing for a workshop and said, "Babe, what if you had never gone to that first vendor sale? You wouldn't be as far along as you are now had you not gone." And, now, I am attending any meeting that time and money will allow! So, my advice is to get yourself out there and get involved!

A virtuous business woman sets a schedule for herself, but allows for flexibility. It is hard to keep an open-ended schedule, but it is something that you might want to think about. It is okay to have normal business or working hours, but there has to be some flexibility there! I will give you an example. My husband and I operate on polar schedules—my business is a day business and his is a night business. I have to account for that more than most because we are also homeschool parents. I have to make sure that my schedule does not keep him from getting the rest that he needs, allows for school with our girls to be done, and does not have him running late for work at night. Do we clash? Yes, and quite hard at times, but we make it work.

Do not over schedule yourself, either. Learn to say no or that you cannot do that right now. I promise you that your business will not fall apart. First and foremost, make sure that you are getting in time with God! I have had my best days when I have taken the time to read the Bible and pray. No matter what it is I read, I find a way to make it relate to my day. I take the time to pray about all that I have before me that particular day. I ask God to help me to make the best decisions possible, to be there when my family needs me, and to do what is right. To many it may seem small and unnecessary, but it most certainly is not. I saw a quote on Facebook that said that if you have not bathed your business in prayer, then you are not ready for profit.

Take care of yourself. We forget that along the way. I remember that I was going so hard and so fast every day that I had a migraine and needed a massage at the end of every day. I was like that for eight months and even lost thirty pounds in the process. I was trying to make sure that everyone had what they needed. I was trying to make sure that I could help my husband. I was trying to make sure that I was doing my absolute best, but I was forgetting about myself. I did not even realize that I was losing the weight. I will spare you the details of how I figured that out. Do not spend more time investing in your business than you do investing in yourself.

A virtuous business woman sets realistic, measureable, and attainable goals with definite and clear deadlines. We all have this pipe dream of what we want our businesses to be, how we want things to run, who we want to be like, who we want to be linked up with, how much money we want to make-- you get the point. What are you doing to get there? Have you even made a plan yet? Have you prayed about it? Did you even write all that stuff down? Yeah, about that!

A virtuous business woman is PIRRPEARed. Do you think I mean prepared? Same thing, but different letters. Let me explain. When it comes to staying relevant in the business world, you have to realize that it is a process! **Pray** about what you are doing and how to keep it going. **Investigate** ways to do what needs to be done without sacrificing way too much. **Read** everything you can get your hands on. **Research** what is new, what still works, what you need to do away with, etc. **Plan** your next course of action. **Execute** the plan you have put together. **Adapt** the plan if necessary. **Re-execute** with the new plan in mind. Does that make sense? You probably never thought about it that way!

Lastly, a virtuous business woman surrounds herself with like-minded people who help her, challenge her, and keep her accountable. That is right, ma'am, you need a TEAM! You need to have those go-to people. These are people that you know you can call and ask for a quick prayer. These are the people you can pitch your ideas to and they will tell you that you need to rethink that. They make sure you are doing what you said you were going to do and pushing you to get off your butt and get your stuff in order—yes, you need them all! The accountability person is by far one of the most important. You need that person who will give you God's answers for the situations that you are facing. You need that person who is not afraid to tell you that what you are doing does not line up with the Bible. You need that. Iron sharpens iron.

Whew! That's was a lot in a little bit. The worksheets for this verse are for you to get PIRRPEARed. It is time to get your life together, honey. Now, go get it!

4 BUILD YOUR BUSINESS BRAIN

Proverbs 31:14—"She is like the merchants' ships; she bringeth her food from afar."

A virtuous business woman looks everywhere for resources to help her business to grow. While you may find what you need in your immediate area, do not be afraid to shop around. There may be something and someone better out there for you to do business with or link up with. I say this to my consulting clients when they are pricing things. I tell them that the publisher or maker of the product may not always have the best prices nor the best deals. The same is true in business. Yes, you may know of someone who can turn your presentation into a New York Times bestseller. However, there may be someone else who can do it quicker. Yes, you will have to pray over your stuff before you send it, but that is a part of doing business.

A virtuous business woman looks at her business from all angles. There is nothing wrong with going back to the drawing board. Remember how I talked about being PIRRPEARed in the last chapter? The A and the R stand for Adapt the plan and Re-execute the plan. Revisit your business mission and vision. Does it need to be expanded? Look at your website. Is it the best representation of you and your business? Look at your blog. Are you posting what is relevant and what people want to read? Look at yourself and how you handle certain aspects of the business. Are there some areas that you need to tighten up in? Where do you and your business stand with God? Is it time to do some recommitting and refocusing? These are things that a virtuous woman thinks about almost on a daily basis. You may be doing well, but you can always do better.

A virtuous business woman carefully considers the source of information given to her and weighs the pros and cons as it applies to the vision and goals for her business.

She makes sure that any information she receives is credible before altering her business model. She makes sure that it makes sense given the scope of her business. She is not quick to join the cause simply because it comes well-advertised and highly recommended. She dissects it because she knows that, if it fails, it is a reflection on her. She takes her time in making the decision and does not allow pushy people who put pressure on her cause her to make a rash decision. She has been there before, in most cases, and is not looking to go there again. The decisions that she has to make could propel her business to the next level or break it back down to ground zero. Not every risk is worth taking.

A virtuous business woman is willing to travel both reasonable and unreasonable distances if it means that what she's looking at is going to propel her business forward. You have been there before. You see a workshop that you know is going to help you solve a problem in your business—and then you see that it is several hours away. You start to think about how you can make it happen because you know you need to be there. You know that the opportunity will probably never be available locally and you really cannot afford to miss it.

You run your numbers and see that you are going to have to get very creative in your spending to allow for travel expenses. Your team will tell you that it is a long way to go for something like that and may even try to show you something similar and closer. You know that is not going to work, so you keep pounding at it until you figure out how to make it work. How do I know? It happened to me.

I was working in a government education program that required us to go through a certain training in our first year on the job. I'd had the job for two years and had not received the training. When my director noticed that there were others as well, he started making moves. There were only two opportunities left: one was in San Juan, Puerto Rico and the other was in the Virgin Islands. I had to make a decision because I would lose my job and the program would lose funding if it was found out that I had never had the training.

I immediately went to my mom and my husband to try to figure out how we could make this work. We had no money for me to travel, so I had to rely on my per diem. All I could think about was losing my job if I did not go to that training. I packed as best I could, called my director, went to the office to make my travel arrangements, and then off I went! Not only did I learn what I needed in order to do my job more efficiently, I had a great time! Although, it was a sacrifice, I had to suck it up. Sometimes the virtuous business woman will find herself in that predicament. Decisions have to be made.

The worksheets for this verse are to help you to make those decisions. There are other scriptures to consider and reflect on as well. Think about what you been told, who has been recommended to you, what you have seen lately, etc. Ask yourself this question: Is this going to help my business and how?

5 CARING FOR THE MULTITUDES

Proverbs 31:15- "She riseth also while it is yet night, and giveth meat to her household, and a portion to her maidens."

A virtuous business woman takes care of her family and her employees, if she has any. Notice that family is first. She takes care of home FIRST, meaning that she makes sure that her family is taken care of and is not second to her business. As hard as that can be, a virtuous business woman knows when she needs to step back and attend to her family.

Recently, I hit a rough patch in my business and found myself with no clientele and pending business expenses. I had also just written my first book, From One King's Daughter to Another, and was scraping for sales. I was so busy running around trying to rebuild my business and deliver books that I was always running out of the house— sometimes multiple times a day.

One evening, my daughter stopped me as I was leaving and asked me how long I would be. It broke my heart! I turned around and apologized to her for being gone so much. She smiled and told me that it was okay because she was starting to understand that having your own business meant being busy. I smiled, hugged her, and left. Once I got back, we sat down together and did some of her favorite things. My husband joined us and held his hand up for silence when I tried to apologize to him. He told me later that he understood that these were things that I had to do in order to get the business running.

Needless to say, I had to slow down and spend time with my family. The next day, I spent almost two hours catching up on my daughter's favorite show—and she was right there with me. I sat down and watched movies and hilarious YouTube videos with my husband. I read books with my other two daughters. THAT was what needed to be done.

I do not have any employees yet, but I will say this—a virtuous business woman treats her employees fairly, pays them competitively, values their work, and rewards and disciplines them with dignity and professionalism. I am going to spend the rest of the chapter breaking those down.

Treating your employees fairly is beyond important! No one wants to work for someone who does not do what they are asking their employees to do. They do not want to work for someone who is always thinking about the workload and their bottom line when they need a little time off from work. They want to work for someone who is approachable. They want to work for someone who does those little things when big events are happening in their lives and understand why those things are important to them. I will give you an example.

One agency that I worked for went overboard with showing how important life events were for their employees. Our birthday was a paid holiday. When someone graduated from college, they received a $25 gift card. When someone had a baby or got married, they received a $50 gift card. When someone was promoted to a higher position, they received a cash gift and something for their new space. When Christmas came around, they received gifts based on how long they had been there. This made the agency easier to work for not only for those reasons, but also because they encouraged their employees to further their education, to go for higher positions, and gave them recommendations that helped them in their pursuits.

A virtuous business woman values the work of her employees. She does not take credit for things and ideas that her employees came up with or created. She gives credit where it is due and shares the spotlight with them. She does not take what they made and not allow them to use it elsewhere. Let me stop right here for a minute because I know some will reread that a million times.

In a job that I had, I created a program that got national attention and I was even nominated for an award. I was getting ready to share it with another organization that was looking for something similar to what I had created and I was told that what I had created became the property of the company where I worked. Any workbooks, lesson outlines, handouts, or anything else I had created became theirs. I could not advertise it, sell it, redistribute it – nothing. While I understood that to be the case for anything created using the program's copyrighted material, I did not like the fact that I had to walk away from what I created and what I had bought to make it possible. I couldn't even recreate it! To this day, my program is still being used and my name has not been mentioned at all. A virtuous business woman would not do this, but would allow that employee to include it in their professional portfolio. You may disagree with that, but I would encourage you to give it some thought. Why? They are not stealing from the company. This is something that they create to use in the company and they should be able to reserve the right to keep it for other uses or receive compensation for it if the company wishes to keep it.

Lastly, a virtuous business woman rewards and disciplines her employees with dignity and professionalism. There are times when things should be done either publicly or privately. An employee should never be discipline publicly. It is okay to talk about what happened in a general sense; however, that person should not be paraded around for everyone to know what happened. It is okay to send out an email entailing what policies and procedures are or will be, but names should not be used.

When it comes to rewarding employees, it should be done as both a reward to them and an encouragement to others. It also should not be excessive, too frequent, nor too flashy. It also needs to be fair! Someone that has been working for you for a year should not get the same thing as someone who has been there from day one. Rewards should have differing, yet fair levels.

This also should not always be done publicly. Not everyone in the company needs to know who earned a bonus. Not everyone in the company needs to know who is getting a raise. Not everyone in the company needs to know who gets a certain position. You have to be careful with making certain things public because it could very well lead to you having issues with disgruntled employees. Be very clear about your expectations for reward and discipline alike.

Always remember that small things mean a lot. Some people do not need much. They just want to know that you know that they are doing their best. A thank you, pat on the back, nice email, or a simple congratulations—these are small things that many will appreciate.

Another thing to remember is that you cannot please everyone. Someone is going to feel that what you are doing as a reward or for discipline is not enough for them. Do not harp too much on what could have happened and what you did not have to do. That will usually add fuel to the fire. Listen to their concerns, take action, and move forward.

The worksheets for this verse are meant to challenge you to get some things right in these areas. The questions are there not only to make you think, but also to make a plan! Do not take the exercises lightly.

6 ESTABLISHING YOUR EMPIRE

Proverbs 31:16- "She considereth a field, and buyeth it: with the fruit of her hands she planteth a vineyard."

A virtuous business woman looks for the perfect place to build her business! She weighs her options of either having her main operation in her home or in a place outside of her home. Sometimes this is a hard decision to make. It really boils down to whether or not you have the space to do so and how you being there will mesh with your family dynamic. Will you be able to work uninterrupted? Will it be quiet around you? Is there an office complex within a reasonable distance of your house? These are decisions I had to make. A virtuous business woman also does not buy or rent the first place she sees! She takes her time, prays about it, and gets the space that is BEST or a stepping-stone toward the best.

I spent the first part of my business journey doing things at night once my kids went to sleep. That made for some very long nights because I knew that I had to get everything I possibly could done. I did my best to set myself up for the next day, yet it did not always work out that way. I would find myself being more tired, sleeping less, and having a headache once I got up.

After we moved, I used my new home as my main base, which did not last long. Why? I fell back into the same habits and then found out that, as a renter, I could not use my home as a business. I had to find an office and fast! I found the first complex two streets over. A virtuous business woman does not buy the biggest space right off and takes care not to put too much on herself in the beginning. That office suite was exactly what I wanted, but that price was not it at all! I found a second place and that did not work out because someone double rented the office. That actually had a happy ending because the property owner made it right by giving me another office in another complex that was one street over from the first place I went to. It was bigger and I was able to get it for the same price as the other one!.

One of the reasons that I chose to agree to the property owner's term was that the rent was an all-inclusive rate! I paid $150 a month and my utilities, printing, copying, faxing, and Wi-Fi access were all included. There was no way I was turning that down!

Once the decision is made – in the home or outside the home—a virtuous business woman fashions that chosen place so that it can be at its best and allow her to serve all whom she meets. Her place is professional, yes, but it is still inviting and decorated for the task. The environment your clients walk into should make them feel at ease in working with you and not make them tenser or doubt that they want to work with you. It should be comfortable and the colors and décor should be as tasteful as possible.

A virtuous business woman is also wary of how much she spends. It is much better to start out with a little and then build on that instead of buying the biggest and the best up front and not having enough money left to run your business. People are surprised today that my husband and I decorated my office with $657.47 – and shopped at Walmart online and our local Family Dollar! It is not necessary to spend thousands of dollars decorating an office!

In her fashioning, a virtuous business woman makes sure that her environment allows for growth to be made and success to be attained. Neither she, her employees (if any), nor her clients should be limited by the size and furnishings in the building. They should walk in there and feel as though they are going to get something done! The artwork on the walls should be inspiring and not just informational. The colors should be intriguing to the eye, but not flashy. When the décor is too out there, people do not take you seriously at all. On the other side of that, a warehouse does not have to look like a warehouse, either! You can jazz up any space if you truly desire to and work at it.

Lastly, she sits down and plans what will go forth from that space. She thinks about what having that space is going to allow her to do. She thinks about the area that she is in and how she can help the community around her by being there. She thinks about whom she will be able to serve to her highest capacity. She contemplates what can and will happen over the course of time.

My challenge for you with this verse is for you to evaluate your current space, if you have one. If you are looking for a space, think about what you need in a space for right now. Use the worksheets for this verse to help you to get that together! Do not forget to plan what can and will happen!

7 MAINTAINING THE WOMAN WITHIN AND WITHOUT

Proverbs 31:17- "She girdeth her loins with strength, and strengtheneth her arms."

A virtuous business woman takes care of herself and keeps up her appearance. She exercises regularly and eats well. This is hard to do, yet it is necessary! She has to be ready at a moment's notice, so it is important that she see after her health. Not only are her clients and employees depending on her, her family is also! She has to make sure that what she puts into her body is the best thing for it and does not cause harm!

A virtuous business woman gets all necessary health checks and exams. I have known business women who have delayed routine and urgent care health matters because of the down time that may result. I am like that myself. What I had to learn was, at the end of the day, when you are not at your best physically, you are not at your best in any other area! A virtuous business woman takes times to herself and recognizes the need to pull back, take a break, and rest. She should have people in place that can take the baton and keep running the race. I know and understand that is not always possible, yet it should be something that she aspires to have. I remember doing sessions by Skype because I had conjunctivitis (pink eye). I remember not asking about having surgery to correct an issue because I was afraid of being bedridden for three to ten weeks. I was more afraid that I was going to get a new client and not be able to serve them. Fortunately, the first line of defense I was given helped just as my doctor and my family hoped it would. That may not always be the case! If you have to do it, do it!

A virtuous business woman's attire is tasteful,

professional, and well made. If you are honest, you have seen business women who you have personally wanted to say something to about the way they were dressed. A truly professionally dressed business woman can sometimes make those who do not take their attire as seriously feel uncomfortable. It should not be that way – on their end. I remember going to an interview once and the man that I was about to be interviewed by came out, saw me, went back into his office, put his tie and jacket back on, came back out, and said, "Now, I feel better." Another time, I was told to dress down for my second interview, which I did. I went from a full business suit to a one-piece dress with flats. When I went back, my interviewer made the comment that she told me to dress down, which I thought I was. It was a test and I passed it! When it comes to being in the business world, a virtuous business woman leads by example!

A virtuous business woman maintains the car she

drives. She does not miss oil changes or service checks. She keeps a full gas tank. She does not push her car to its limits and think that she can buy more time. She has full insurance on the car she drives. She keeps her driving record clear. She makes sure the tags are current. She keeps up with car payments. She has roadside assistance, AAA, and a reliable car rental company should anything happen. She keeps the car clean, inside and out. She understands the difference between personal and business mileage while maintaining proper records. She understands that her vehicle is a reflection of her! I do not think I have any more to say about that!

A virtuous business woman is in tune with God and has a solid and stable support system. She realizes the importance of having God in her corner and honoring Him! She lets nothing and no one stop her from having her quiet time with God and is known as a woman of prayer and fasting if need be! She remembers that the ultimate goal is to please God in all that she does. She realizes that she has to stand before God and give an account of her life, her home, and her business. She makes sure that everything she does is lined up with what God requires. She surrounds herself with like-minded people who will not only help her professionally, but also will point her back to God when it is necessary. She surrounds herself with those who challenge her to do more, go further, and push harder. She surrounds herself with those that will help her to keep her head together, but not make her feel as though she is doing everything wrong. I know how that feels.

My mom, God rest her soul, was the worst at playing Devil's Advocate. She wanted me to succeed and do as much as I could in life, but she shot down everything that I ever wanted to do. I either was not strong enough, did not know enough, was not tough or firm enough, or just plain flat out couldn't do it! It got to the point to where I could not even tell her what I was doing. I had to find others that provided more of a balance for me. I was not looking for anyone to blow sunshine at me, but I knew I needed someone who could see what I was capable of and help me to work toward making things better. That brings me to my last point for this chapter.

A virtuous business woman spends time strengthening her weak points. She is teachable—this goes back to where we talked about a virtuous woman educating herself. She recognizes what she needs help with and asks for it! Whether it is taking care of herself, managing the business, maintaining her vehicle, or even something as simple as creating a social media post—she either researches how to best do it herself or she enlists the help of others. She does not keep up appearances and fakes as if she knows what she is doing, either. She acknowledges what she does not know and sets out to learn so that will never happen again!

I know how it feels to not be able to do something. It is not a great feeling; however, having a pity party about it and constantly talking about what I could not do was not going to get it done. Neither was wishing that I did knew how to do it. It was time to roll my sleeves up, get on my computer, and figure it out. Now, I cannot remember not being able to do it!

For this chapter's exercises, I want you to focus on what you are NOT doing and make plans to start going it. That is the purpose of the worksheets for this verse!

8 HAVING A GO-GETTER MENTALITY

Proverbs 31:18- "She perceiveth that her merchandise is good: her candle goeth not out by night."

A virtuous business woman knows the value of the products and services she offers, but is always looking for ways to improve and serve more people. This means that she stands by the services she provides and can back them up with reputable success stories. She stands by the prices she sets, no matter who may think they are too high or too low. She shows her clients what they will get for the price that they are being asked to pay. This means that the ideas that she presents are original and not the work of someone else – she is not a thief! And, if by chance she IS using someone else's material or ideas, she gives them credit for allowing her to do so. That is where lawsuits and damaged relationships are bred and spiral out of control. It is better to create and have our own! Trust me.

A virtuous business woman keeps up with what her competition – if she has any—is doing and adapts without putting herself in the hole. She does not allow the demon of comparison to be fed. She needs to understand that what she has created is good enough to stand toe to toe with what is already out there. She updates her products and services based on market trends that match her core values, the needs of her clients, and newfound knowledge.

A virtuous business woman is not afraid to approach her competition and see how they are able to help each other. She believes in networking, even if it is with someone who is in direct competition with her. She understands that sometimes even rivals can help each other. She forms viable and lucrative partnerships after doing her homework on them. She is well informed and well educated about her competition and what they do. She finds those that compliment her services and vice versa.

A virtuous business woman works late when it is necessary, especially at the beginning! She sets herself up for success on a daily basis. She makes sure that she has everything she needs to make things happen. That means that those important emails are sent and responses are done. That means that she has made her office supply order. That means that she has planned things out, no matter how loose the plans are. That means that she has confirmed any outside arrangements made with time enough to put plan B into action if necessary.

A virtuous business woman sets and maintains high standards and expectations in her business dealings. She comes to the table with her best, not with day old leftover scraps. She puts her best foot forward every day she steps into the workplace. She is ready for whatever comes her way. She expects nothing less than the best out of herself and her employees. She also has a right to have reasonably high expectations of others she has business dealings with, yet understands that those expectations will not always be met. She understands that not everyone she deals with will have the same values and work ethic as she does. I have had that to happen myself.

I was interested in starting a business relationship with someone and I was ready to go! I had all of my ideas laid out and I knew that what I had would be a real game changer for the both of us. I pitched my ideas to this other person and she was excited. However, when it came time to get started with the planning process, she always had an excuse as to why she could not do things on the day and time that we set. I sent her things by both email and regular mail that she never did anything with, so I went on and started working on other things. Something told me to check in and see what was going on. I have not been able to contact her! While I was upset, I had to realize that she simply was not ready. I had to let that go because I could not afford to spend time chasing her down. I moved on! While it was not an easy decision to make, it needed to be made nonetheless. I do not harbor any ill feelings toward her either. That shows maturity!

A virtuous business woman connects with people who can help her and vice versa. Learning to both give and accept help is important. Whether your business is well established or you are just starting out, it is important to network throughout every stage of your business. I did this while building my coaching business. I went to networking events and presented myself and my business to everyone in there that I knew could help propel my business forward. I explained that, although I had just started, I believed in networking while I built. I ended up with a workshop spot, several speaking engagements, and interest in the book I had written a month earlier. It is important to let the right people know what you are doing because they can help you more than you think they can.

For example, I had been looking for a particular individual for several months and I ended up seeing her at a community event. I asked the person next to me if that was the person I was looking for and they told me that it was and that I needed to go and talk to her. I quickly packed up my booth and went to do just that. This may sound cliché, but I was glad that I did. In that instance, I ended up with a workshop spot, a discount on advertising for my business, and she came to an event that I did a couple of weeks later!

Another time, I had lunch with a lady that I met while attending an event with my brother, who is also an author and entrepreneur. We bounced ideas off each other and really connected. I was thinking about giving her a copy of my latest book and then she said that she was looking for a book for the girls that she was working with. I smiled and slid the book across the table. Both of us started laughing! She read the first page and asked me if I had any more.

I told all of those stories so that you could see how important it is to link up with those that you know will help further my goals as a virtuous business woman. I understood that I did not have to have it all together in order to do that. I understood that it would eventually help me to get things in order as they needed to be.

A virtuous business woman is always looking for opportunities! She pays attention to what she sees and hears around her. She speaks up at the right time and is always ready to do so. She is prepared to start working with someone immediately should that be the case. Her preparedness can sometimes be seen as intimidating or even slightly annoying, but her purpose in being that way always becomes clear. She wants whomever she may be speaking with to see that she is the right person to be dealing with in that situation. As I mentioned before, she attends both business and community events where she can get her message out, get her products seen, and potentially get her calendar full. It should get to the point to where she is usually expected to show up at certain events. It should be a shock that she is not there. That comes from people knowing her and what her business is about!

In looking for opportunities, though, a virtuous business woman knows that not every opportunity presented to her is one that she should seize. She prays about any opportunity she's considering and does not jump on the first train of the day. She does her homework. She understands that her reputation is on the line and that she cannot be seen working and networking with any and every body out there. Have I ever refused to work with someone? Yes, I have.

It was one of those times when the opportunity

seemed to simply be too perfect. I decided to attend an event where I thought I would learn a lot of valuable information. I rearranged my family schedule so that I could attend this event. After only a few minutes of being there, I realized that it was more about increasing their numbers than it was about giving information. I did not go to the next meeting. It was not what I was looking for or looking to be involved in.

A virtuous business woman is a go-getter. She does not wait around for things to come to her. She keeps her ear to the ground and does for herself. She realizes that attitude just might be the driving force behind her getting things done. She knows that things are not going to just fall into her lap. She is going to have to put the work in for what she wants. Yes, she may get a little less sleep. Yes, she may have many headaches. However, she does what is right, pleasing before God, and necessary to get things done.

For this verse's exercises, I want you to think about whether or not you have this particular quality. I want you to think about how you exhibit it if you do. If you are not there just yet, make a plan of how you are going to get there and make things happen. A virtuous business woman may take her time, but she also knows that time waits for no one!

9 SHINING THE LIGHT

Proverbs 31:19- "She layeth her hands to the spindle, and her hands hold the distaff."

A virtuous business woman does things for herself, if she has to, in order to keep her business going! She is very careful with how much she outsources. While outsourcing is necessary, it can be overdone and can become very expensive and more time consuming! She learns how to do what she needs to do when money is an issue. She knows what is out there, but she also knows that she needs to keep her bottom line in tact as well. She will barter should that be feasible, but not every single time she needs something!

A virtuous business woman is industrious and hardworking. She is always busy and it may seem to some that she never takes an off day, even when she is taking one! Having a business takes work—work that has to be done by her no matter what. She is not one to take the easy way out and believes in making her work smarter and not harder. She does things in a way that makes her next steps easier to take. She is a woman that believes in and understands the importance of preparation. She gives twice as much effort as she expects to receive. She is often criticized for doing too much, yet she knows that it needs to get done. She is intentionally over prepared.

I will tell you this—I am a chronic over preparer. I actually had someone to tell me once that I was too ready for the event of the day. I was at a vendor sale and I went in ready to sell! I had both of my cell phones out with the card readers attached. I was signed into both of my payment systems and even had my iPad and laptop ready should anything go down. I had everything with me, too. If someone wanted to schedule a meeting after purchasing what

I had, I was ready to give them what they needed to take that next step. I go into meetings and events prepared for people to say yes, but they do not know that until the yes is communicated.

A virtuous business woman is both detail and task oriented. She pays attention to the smallest of details and breaks big projects down into manageable tasks with deadlines attached. She makes sure that every T is crossed and every I is dotted. She makes sure that she is prepared for anything that could go wrong. She is thorough, which can be seen as too much for some.

I was preparing for a client meeting at my home, which I do not normally do. I knew my client would be there for several hours, as she wanted everything I had to offer. So, I set out to prepare my home for this meeting. First, I made sure that my kids were bedded down for the night. Next, I made sure that my home was clean and fresh smelling. I even broke out the lavender essential oils plugins! Then, I set up a space for my client to work. I made sure that my most comfortable chair was available and ready. I set out supplies that I thought would be useful—notebooks, pens, pencils, highlighters, and erasers. Last, I made a snack basket complete with ice-cold juice and water.

Why did I do all that? I knew that this client would be at my home for several hours. Was it intimidating for the client? Yes, it was; however, everything I put out was used and eaten! I saw it as being attentive to the potential needs of my client. I wanted to make sure that they had everything that was needed to complete the tasks for the evening.

In being detail and task oriented, a virtuous business woman makes sure that she does her absolute best. She checks, double checks, and triple checks any written communication that she is sending out to people. She makes sure it is not too wordy, is easy to understand, that it communicates exactly what it needs to, and that it serves the right purpose. She makes sure that it is both eye-catching and appealing, yet still maintains the proper professional tone. She makes sure that she is not being demeaning or condescending in getting her point across. People should be both impressed and informed with anything that they receive from her. What she presents is straightforward and has no gray areas.

A virtuous business woman is not afraid to pound the pavement in order to get her name out there. She looks for both traditional and untraditional means of exposure without compromising whom she is and what she is trying to get done. I was talking about this in a Facebook group for entrepreneurs. I suggested that we should not rely solely on social media and email to advertise our businesses. Why? There are people that you will not reach that way. A select few in the world still value letters, flyers, and cards. They would much rather get a phone call than a text message.

With that being said, a virtuous business woman makes sure that her message gets out across a myriad of avenues. She scouts out the best places to leave information about her business and what she is trying to do. She follows advertising protocols and does not assume that she can put her information out anywhere and everywhere. I have gotten phone calls about leaving information in certain places without asking. Be careful with that!

A virtuous business woman makes sure that she stays ahead of the game. She knows what is happening, when, where, how, and who to contact. She makes sure that she is financially ready to get vendor space at events. She makes sure that her marketing materials are noticeable and draw people to her. She is not afraid to offer incentives for working with her, but she does not give too much away for free. She gives just enough to attract and keep interest.

A virtuous business woman knows how to use the tools of her particular trade. She knows her way around a computer. She knows what apps work best for her and she is beyond proficient in using them. She knows how to use any tools and machines that she is around. She always has the best and the latest that is related to her business and understands the value of upgrading when it is time to do so. She does her research throughout the process of using anything. She looks for tools that will lead to her being more productive. As previously stated, she makes sure that she has all necessary supplies. If she finds herself in a time crunch, she knows where to go to get things done in the time needed.

A virtuous business woman's sleeves are always rolled up and she is ready to work at any given time. When there is a crisis, a big deadline, or a big event coming, the virtuous business woman prays to God for help and strength and then she puts her hands on something. She is known as someone who is willing to work hard, is willing to step in and help, is both dependable and reliable, and sets the bar high when it comes to working and helping others.

For this chapter and verse's exercise, I want you to think about where you are right now. Would these things be said of you? What is stopping that from happening? What can you do to rectify that? Take this time to really think about that.

10 BEING OTHERS MINDED

Proverbs 31:20—"She stretcheth her hand to the poor; yea, she reacheth forth her hand to the needy."

A virtuous business woman looks for ways to help the community through her business without giving too much away. Did we not talk about this already? Yes, but this time we are going to look at it from a different angle.

A virtuous business woman prayerfully participates in events hosted by organizations that she supports. Her affiliations are clear, as are her reasons for having those affiliations. This is a two-edged sword at times because there will be someone somewhere who will take issue with who and what she chooses to support; however, she cannot allow that to influence her. As we said before, it is not meant for us to work and link up with everyone we encounter. Not every cause is one that we should support. She is criticized for supporting organizations that may be seen as old-fashioned, outdated, and antiquated. She may be accused of being close-minded and told that she needs to broaden her spectrum of thinking.

On the other hand, there will be those who are glad to have her supporting and endorsing them. These organizations are looking for people who are not scared to go against the grain and stick with those causes and organizations that are time tested and approved. She is not quick to support something new, either. She has to see results before putting her name behind it. She realizes that whom she allows herself to affiliate with can make her or break her in some instances. She is also not afraid to lose clientele that take issue with who she supports. She supports those that line up with her business convictions and values. More importantly, she supports those that line up with God!

A virtuous business woman is visible, involved, and vocal in the communities surrounding both her home and her business. People know and are comfortable with her and know that she will stand for what is right, even when that position is unpopular. She is known as someone who speaks up for those who cannot speak up for themselves and holds those in power around her accountable. She does her part in making the community safe. Her neighbors and colleagues are happy to know her. She is approachable and takes time to listen to the concerns of those that come to her for help. She is able to recognize something out of the ordinary and take action without endangering herself.

A virtuous business woman volunteers her time when things happen. Not every problem can be solved while sitting behind a desk! She puts on that company t-shirt (or not) and goes to where she is needed. She does not show up emptyhanded, either. She may not know exactly what is needed, but she walks into the situation with something in hand. She is ready to help, even if the work is going to be hard.

I remember helping a friend with the city's Thanksgiving Dinner for the homeless. I was up at 4 a.m. headed downtown to the convention center where the event was taking place. I brought a few more people with me because I was not sure if more bodies would be needed. I deboned turkeys. I stirred dressing in vats the size of my car. I cut up massive amounts of cranberry sauce. I cleaned up, came out of the kitchen, and helped serve. I stayed around to help clean up for the next wave. I went back to the kitchen to see if I was still needed and was willing to stay even though I had already been there for six hours straight. Later on that day, the news ran a ticker across the bottom of the screen giving shout outs to all that came to help. My name was there.

I remember my days of working in high schools when Hurricane Katrina hit and kids started pouring in to the area. I wanted to do something more than just bottled water, so I went to the store, and bought 20 backpacks, school supplies to fill them, and as many school uniforms as I could get my hands on. I tied my agency's business card to each one. For the kids who were graduating seniors, I had fee waivers for them to use in order to apply to my alma mater, Christian Brothers University, if I found that they qualified.

I did not bring all of that up to brag. I did it to show what you can do in your community to help! The smallest gestures can lead to better and greater later. Think about that as you complete the worksheets for this chapter and verse. How are you seen in your community?

11 MAKE WAY FOR THE BEST

Proverbs 31:21—"She is not afraid of the snow for her household: for all her household are clothed with scarlet."

Now, we are going to approach this one two ways: family and business, with family being first. A virtuous business woman makes sure that when the seasons change, her family is prepared for it. Her children have good, sturdy cold weather clothing that fits. They have hats, gloves, and whatever else is needed to help them during the winter months. She makes sure that what they are eating gives them energy and is filling. She scouts out alternative routes to get them to school and stays on top of school closings. If she homeschools her children, she makes sure that they have everything they need at home to continue their learning. She keeps an eye on sensitive areas at home and sees that they are protected.

Now for the business part. A virtuous business woman has her employees in a safe and comfortable working environment with thought for the weather. She has a fair inclement weather policy and does not expect her employees to brave hazardous conditions to get to work. She makes a way for them to work from home if possible. She checks in on them and their families to make sure that they are okay and have what they need. When the summer months come, she makes sure to limit the time they are outside and is aware of heat advisories. If they have to be outside, she makes sure that they stay fed, stay hydrated, and take needed breaks.

The building that the virtuous business woman's employees work in is well maintained and prepared for the weather. When her employees come to work, it is not the same temperature in the building as it is outside. They are able to work at their highest productivity levels because they are comfortable. When there is a severe weather threat, her employees are able to find a place of safety and are allowed to check on their loved ones. She provides for them if they end up being shut in or locked down for any reason.

A virtuous business woman provides weather appropriate uniforms for those that need it and a flexible, yet professional, dress code for others. The uniforms that she provides are well made and hold up to the weather. They are not too thick nor too thin. She has her employees' best interest at heart. She makes sure that what she provides will help them to do their job to the best of their ability.

A virtuous business woman makes sure that the vehicles and tools that her employees use are ready for the weather as well! She makes sure that nothing is going to break down because it was not properly maintained. Anyone who drives a company vehicle will have air and heat in the vehicle. They will not have to worry about breaking down somewhere because vehicle maintenance was not done.

A virtuous business woman has happy employees. They enjoy working for her because they know that they matter to her. They are willing to give extra effort because she shows them that they are valuable to her. They feel as though she is in tune with what they need and does not expect them to do anything that she would not do. She takes care of those who are injured or have weather related incidents to occur. They know she will not expect them to keep working through a weather related health issue. She will get them the medical attention that is necessary!

There is not too much more I can say here, so I will leave you to the worksheet for this chapter. Think about the policies that you have in place in your business. If they are not in place, it is time to make a plan. If you have a plan that is not working, it is time to revamp that plan. Do not be afraid to ask your employees what they need to get their jobs done during those weather changes.

12 YOU ARE WHAT YOU WEAR

Proverbs 31:22- "She maketh herself coverings of tapestry; her clothing is silk and purple."

A virtuous business woman has a flexible wardrobe and dresses for the occasion at hand. She does not show up to a community clean up event in a business suit and heels! Her clothing is well made and not too flamboyant. She knows when to dress up, dress down, or dress to the nines!

A virtuous business woman is conscious of what she wears at all times. She does not wear certain things to work simply because she can. She realizes that she has set expectations and abides by them herself. She does not come to work in something that violates policy. Again, she leads by example. She also watches how she wears her hair. The whole point of this is to say that she does not draw unnecessary attention to herself. The way that she looks should not be the sole focus of the day.

A virtuous business woman dresses with a sense of modesty, dignity, sophistication, and professionalism. We can all come up with an example of someone coming to work in something they should not have worn in a work environment. She should not change because people around her are uncomfortable, either. She should serve as an example to those around her.

One thing that I was told in a workshop once was that, if you doubted how you were supposed to dress for a job, watch your boss. A virtuous business woman should be someone who those under her can pattern themselves after in this area. You can go overboard with it, so be careful. How can you go overboard? I will tell you.

A virtuous business woman would not expect her employees to dress in the same way she does. Let me explain. While she might make recommendations or give advice, she has to understand that they may not be possible for all of her employees. They may not make enough to shop where she shops. The material she wears may not look the same way on them. The color she wears may not be right for them. This is what happens when you have unrealistic expectations.

A virtuous business woman does not have a double standard in her dress. We have talked about that some already, but let us go a little further. She does not have the "'Do as I say and not as I do" mentality with her employees. Again, she does not wear something that violates the policy that she put in case nor does she reprimand someone that does the same on the same day. In other words, she cannot come to work in fishnet stockings and then tell another employee that she has to go home and change. Nine times out of ten that employee is going to call her out as well. Her response should not be that she is the boss and she can do what she wants. That causes confusion and then people start to think that way every time they see her.

Double standards are dangerous in business and in other areas as well! A virtuous business woman cannot come in looking as though she stepped off a magazine cover while her employees barely have what they need, when the uniforms are company issued, in order to be in accordance with the dress code. That tells her employees that she is more important than they are and that they will just have to deal with that they are given. Having that kind of mentality breeds contempt and leads to low productivity among employees. It also causes a breakdown in the employer-employee relationship.

I know some have tried to account for this by having a separate dress code policy for management level and entry-level employees. Even with that in mind, a virtuous business woman still watches what she wears and should not have a bad attitude about someone telling her she could be take more care in what she chose to wear on a particular day.

I have seen it too many times! Differences were made when they should not have been made. A virtuous business woman does not use her position to excuse her actions, her dress, her work ethic, or her demeanor. I am going to leave you with that.

My challenge to you in this chapter is to take a good long look at yourself and what you have in your closet. Ask yourself what you would do if an employee came to work dressed as you were. Be objective in that, too, and be honest. Although you are in a higher position, you are being watched just as you are watching others.

13 HER EMPIRE—HIS EMPIRE

Proverbs 31:23- "Her husband is known in the gates, when he sitteth among the elders of the land."

A virtuous business woman uses her business to help exalt her husband. Huh? She does WHAT? Let me explain. She creates opportunities for her husband to use his skills in her business and gives him credit for his contributions. Even though the business is "yours," there should be allowances for him to contribute. You know what he can do. You know what he is good at. Give him the chance to flex his muscles and show his skills.

For example, the credit for decorating my office goes to my husband! I bought one picture! I also give him credit for helping me make presentations and marketing materials look more appealing and succinct. When people I interact with meet him, they already know about him and that has led to side opportunities for him. Think about that for a second.

A virtuous business woman may have her husband as her first client, depending on the scope of her business. She is doing more than bouncing ideas off of him – she is helping him to start something of his own or helping him in the job that he currently has. She uses what she has learned to help him to get ahead in what he is doing. This reminds me of my mentor. Her husband has his own business, but she does all of his branding and marketing, which is one of the things she does in her business. He was her first client!

Again, a virtuous business woman uses her skills to help her husband build his entrepreneurial dreams. She is not stingy with what she learns nor does she treat him differently from any other client. Yes, she is dealing with her husband, but he should receive the same level of effort that she would give another client. The only difference that should exist is whether she charges him or not, which is between the two of them. She realizes that in helping him, she is also helping herself. Her husband can help her to fine tune her pitches, revise her approach, and come up with new ideas. This should be the safest client relationship of all! This should be the most fulfilling. This one should get the most effort.

My husband loves coaching sports. Since I am always creating some kind of binder, handbook, or booklet, I helped him create his own baseball coaching manual. I helped with editing, proofreading, and picking graphics. That is just an example of how I use something that I do in my business to help him.

A virtuous business woman is supportive of her husband's career and entrepreneurial pursuits, which can sometimes cause a conflict. However, she and her husband should find common ground so that neither one of them is forced to give up what they are doing for the sake of the other. This is not an easy thing to do! Schedules get crossed, emergencies come up, and things happen. That is why it is important that the virtuous business woman makes sure that she and her husband stay on the same page at all times.

A virtuous business woman has her husband's best business interests at heart. She does not do anything to undermine his business nor intentionally bring it down. She does not allow his business successes to make her jealous and cloud her judgment. She does not refuse to help him if things are moving faster and doing better in his business than in hers at the time. She does not refer him to subpar people to get business needs met. She does not withhold information that will keep him from making a bad business decision. She does not leave him on his own. She does small things behind the scenes to help him, even when he does not want her to and says he has it together. She pays attention to the things he looks over and makes sure that it is not needed. She does not say that she does not have time to help him because she is too busy.

As hard as it may be, a virtuous business woman realizes that his career or entrepreneurship is just as important as hers is and that he deserves the same – if not more—support than he gives her. She understands that it is not all about her and is willing to share the stage with her husband without feeling as if she is being slighted. She makes it her business to professionally coexist with her husband. She prays for him and his business. She recommends him to those who may need him. She lets him know about events that are going on that are relevant to him. She helps him to keep his calendar straight, among other things. She makes sure that whatever she does for her business, she does for his! When he has a special event, she is there and gives her undivided attention and effort. At that moment, she is all about him and what he has going on. She is the epitome of a strong united front for him.

Your exercise for this challenge is simple—think about how you can help your husband! Use the worksheet provided to help you come up with a plan!

14 ESTABLISHING YOUR REPUTATION

Proverbs 31:24- "She maketh fine linen, and selleth it; and delivereth girdles unto the merchant."

A virtuous business woman always has quality products, inventory on hand, and is ready to sell at a moment's notice. This is something that resonates with me so much! I was giving my first workshop and something told me to bring my rolling cart with me and not to take anything out of it. I was glad that I listened. Why? There was a lady there who had just started homeschooling and needed activities for her son. Guess what was in the cart— all of the lesson plans and learning tools that I had recently created! Not only was I able to give the lady valuable information during the workshop, she left with something to start with and that made me feel amazing!

A virtuous business woman is prepared to both talk about and demonstrate her product or service. She is knowledgeable about what she offers and speaks about it in a way that earns her a client contract or sale. She is not pushy, obnoxious, or forceful, nor does she appear to be a know-it-all. She knows how to present her business and skill set with confidence and professional decorum. She watches her body language when communicating with a potential client. She mentally checks her attitude and her demeanor as well. She is conscious of how she is coming across in the conversation and is willing to quickly correct herself when needed. Her goal is to make sure that the person talking to her leaves the conversation with a good vibe about her.

A virtuous business woman delivers her products quickly and promptly. That means that her clients get what they were promised, when they were promised, how they were promised, and at the price they were promised. She is not one to risk her professional reputation over being tired, overconfident, nor complacent. She takes every order and appointment seriously. Her clients know her as someone who does what she says she is going to do. She stays in constant communication with everyone involved to insure that things are handled properly and takes care of it when it is not.

A virtuous business woman makes she that she has enough supplies for whatever she is endeavoring to do. She knows who, what, when, where, why, how, and how much. She has a backup plan when she does not have access to her go-to people. She has done her homework and develops tunnel vision when it is necessary. She focuses on the task that hand and is not easily distracted. She sometimes over prepares on purpose!

When I had my first speaking engagements, I was told to prepare for thirteen at one site and twelve at the other. I could not see myself preparing for only twenty-five people, so I prepared for fifty-three. I had almost forty people combined! I remember my husband and me smiling about how we had gone back and forth about how many to prepare for. This is definitely one instance where I was glad to be over prepared.

Getting back to the matter at hand, a virtuous business woman orders necessary items in a timely manner. She doesn't look at her planner, see an event coming up, and say that she doesn't have to do it today because she has time. A statement like that will be her undoing. Why? It is because things happen! The item she needs may be backordered. A storm system could come in that would delay her order. Worst of all, what she orders could not arrive until after the event for which it was needed! This is not a chance that a virtuous business woman takes. If she has any doubt at all, she does something about that. She calls the merchant to make sure that it is in stock and does not rely on what she sees on their website. She checks with shipping companies to see if there is anything going on that could delay her order. She, again, has a plan B should she not be able to do things the exact way that she planned! Think about that for a minute.

A virtuous business woman has people in place to help ensure that things are done properly. She knows that sometimes being a one-woman show is just not possible, feasible, or healthy! She knows whom she can count on and she compensates them fairly. She does not undervalue them. She refuses to allow them to work for free. She takes care of them. She listens to them and realizes that they are there to help and not to change everything about her business. She understands that they are there so that all she has to do is serve her clients and not worry about all the behind the scenes stuff.

I recently became this person for my brother. Anytime he has a speaking engagement that involves book sales, I am there. He hates it when I do that, but I do not care! He knows that all I want him to do is walk in the door, speak, and sign the books that have been purchased. What do I do? I make sure that there are no blank spots on the table. I make sure that I stay logged in to his payment software and that the connection is strong where I am. I have my laptop and iPad out and on his author's page on Amazon for those who want to order their books online. Does he take care of me? Yes, he does! How? He speaks up for me while I'm busy working, meaning that he lets people know who I am, what I do, and that I'm an author as well. He lets me know about upcoming events that are relevant to me. If someone comes to him that he cannot help, he will send them my way. Not to mention he pays for gas, parking, food, and my time! Would your team say this about you?

A virtuous business woman trains her employees well enough to be able to speak in her stead! I cannot stress enough how important this is!

"I don't know" should never be a part of any of your team members' or employees' vocabulary. She makes sure that they can answer questions about her products and services. They should not have to run to her for help with answering simple questions. They should only have to come to her when it is a matter that everyone knows that she needs to handle. For example, I help a friend with her bakery business. I know all of her policies and procedures and I only call her for price quotes! However, when I get a call for a wedding cake, I refer them to her because that is a major part of her business and I do not want to mess anything up. However, she trusts me to take care of other customer calls that come in on the line.

A virtuous business woman follows up with clients and takes care of issues promptly. This is major when it comes to client relationships. Her clients want to know that they will not be abandoned once the money is paid and the service is done. They want to know that she is going to check on them and offer additional assistance in the future or just to find out how things are going. For example, I check on my clients every two weeks!

Think about this as you work on the exercises for this chapter and verse. Think about what you need to revamp, revise, or improve!

15 BE YOUR OWN REWARD

Proverbs 31:25-"Strength and honour are her clothing; and she will rejoice in time to come."

A virtuous business woman does not need constant recognition in order to feel successful. She focuses on both the work and the reward. She realizes that sometimes the work itself is the reward! She understands and sees the value in a smiling customer's face. The feeling that comes from knowing that she has given them what they need can be just as fulfilling.

A virtuous business woman understands that results are not always immediate! Although it can be frustrating, she knows that things can take more time and more effort. She understands that she may have a client that she never hears from again, but she will see something about them later on that will make her smile. She understands that she may have only been a seed planter to that client. They got what they needed from her for the moment and went on to work with someone else. However, she can still rejoice because it all started with her. This principle was very evident in the life of the Apostle Paul! I Corinthians 3:6,7 says-" I have planted, Apollos watered, but God gave the increase. So then neither is he that planted any thing, neither he that watereth; but God that giveth the increase." The virtuous business woman understands that and is able to move forward without any resentment.

A virtuous business woman knows that not every encounter will turn into a business deal or sale. We just talked about that! She is not meant to work with everyone and not everyone is meant to work with her. She understands that she offers something of value, yet not to everyone. I hear people say all the time that they were not a good fit for someone. The same is true for the virtuous business woman. Although this may be the case, she goes a step further and refers them to someone who may be a better fit for them. She does not just leave them to their own devices. She still helps.

A virtuous business woman does not work in order to be considered for awards or memberships in professional organizations. She does not dismiss these things, yet she realizes there is much more at stake. She works in spite of and seeks to please the Lord before anyone else! Although she may be judged unfairly by not being affiliated with certain organizations, she does not jump up and apply just to gain clientele. Remember how we talked about the virtuous business woman prayerfully considering whom she links up with? This is what I mean. And, it is important to note that some of these so-called "professional organizations" are not worth their name. Some of them are simply looking to recruit and have nothing real to offer. Some even go so far as to ask that you pay for the award that they say you "won." The virtuous business woman does not fall for that.

A virtuous business woman knows that her day is coming and looks to God to open doors for her! She knows how important it is to do things in God's timing, that promotion comes from Him, and that it will come so long as she is doing what is right and pleasing before Him. She also knows the difference between what comes from God and what does not. She does not fall for every good thing that comes towards her. She recognizes when things come with strings attached. She knows when things are too good to be true. She pays attention to what has happened to others who have gone down that road. She is not easily attracted by notoriety.

A virtuous business woman knows how to be her own reward! Think about it. Think about the day that you met all of the goals and deadlines that you had and how good you felt about it. You wanted to do a little something for yourself and there is nothing wrong with that. You maybe left early that day or took a much needed and deserved vacation. You may go to eat at a restaurant that you have wanted to try out. You bought yourself something you had your eye on. Or, you did something for the business that you had been putting off because you were so busy. You maybe even did something for someone else! The possibilities are fun to consider and endless. She is her own motivation. She is her own cheering squad. And, she is okay with that!

As you work through the exercises for this chapter and verse, think about what rewards drive you. Think about what you would want. Think about what you would do for yourself when given the chance. Think about the doors that God has opened you!

16 KEEP YOURSELF IN CHECK

Proverbs 31:26- "She openeth her mouth with wisdom; and in her tongue is the law of kindness."

A virtuous business woman not only knows what she's talking about, but also knows how to talk to people! We can all remember a time when we have not liked the way in which someone spoke to us. It was not what they said – it was how they said it. A virtuous business woman watches how she speaks to people. She does not talk down to people as if they are beneath her. I have had this happen to me and had to watch how I responded. She does not speak to people as if they know nothing of what she's talking about. She will be surprised the moment that she does because she just may find out something about the subject that she did not know.

A virtuous business woman knows how to agree to disagree without taking it personally. This is something that many business woman struggle with—disagreement. We are prone to see it as something that we did or said wrong that caused the situation to end as it did. She understands that not everyone will see things her way, no matter how right she may be. She may know that she is right. Those to whom she is speaking may know she is right, yet that does not mean that they are going to admit it, either. She knows how to gracefully and tactfully end any disagreement and is mindful of her emotions and tone as well.

A virtuous business woman can keep her composure under pressure. She is not hot headed nor quick tempered. She can sometimes be seen as nonchalant and uncaring, which is not the case at all. She knows how to handle herself and deals with her personal feelings in private. No one in the room will know that she is shaken unless it is something dire. Even then, she is able to remain poised and level headed, which is not an easy thing to do at all, but she learns how to do it.

A virtuous business woman is an active listener. She listens to understand and not to rebut or respond. We have all had times where we have started responding to what someone said only to have them to tell us that we were not listening to what they said. A virtuous business woman listens and considers everything that is said to her before she answers. People will think that she is not listening; that is, until she responds! She allows the speaker to finish their complete thought and then asks them if they are done speaking. It is then that she communicates her side of the issue with tact, respect, and clarity. She makes sure that she is not misunderstood.

A virtuous business woman speaks to build up and not to tear down. This is very important for any business woman that has employees. She knows how to get her point across and it not be mistaken as harsh. That comes from having a good rapport with those she employs, yet it is not an easy thing to establish. She can deliver bad news in a good way and still maintain the integrity of the relationship. She may even over explain why it is being said and what needs to be done after it has been said. She does that because she wants the person to still feel as though they are a vital part of the organization. Does this apply to terminating someone also? Yes, it does. She knows how to point out the reason for the termination without making it personal and without attacking the person. When she is asked about this person, she does not automatically begin to speak negatively of them. She highlights what they did that worked well while she employed them and discusses the issues that they had in a professional tone.

A virtuous business woman maintains a professional demeanor in her speech and communication. She knows when to be serious and when to be laid back. She respects the position of the person to whom she is speaking. For example, she does not speak to an elected official as if he or she was someone she met on the street, even if she knows them personally. She does not use a lot of slang when speaking to people. The fact that she endeavors to speak properly at all times can annoy people who are not used to that. She would much rather be known as someone who is articulate.

A virtuous business woman is clear in what she says and makes sure it is understood. If she is a mother, she already knows how this goes. She knows that there will be people who are not really listening while she is talking. She will then say something that she knows will bring them back into the conversation. She will purposely ask the same question ten different ways to make sure that she is being understood. She will send an email reminding the listeners of what was talked about previously. She will repeat herself when necessary and will not care that people are annoyed by it. She may even go so far as to record herself in case of a chronic misunderstanding.

A virtuous business woman is not easily drawn into drama and frivolous arguments. She understands that she does not have to get involved in every conversation that comes her way. She can sense when to back away from a conversation. She stays out of conversations she should not be involved in. She recognizes when she needs to intervene. She is capable of keeping business and personal matters separate and addresses them at the appropriate times.

A virtuous business woman thinks before she speaks. She questions what she is about to say. She makes sure that she is going to say it in the best possible way. She thinks about whether or not it should even be said. She plans how she is going to say it, especially if she is upset. She is laughed at because she has often seen talking to herself. She knows that she needs to do that in order to keep her head straight. She prays and asks God for wisdom and guidance in what to say and how to say it, which takes us into the exercise for this verse.

Think about ways you can communicate better. Do those to whom you speak see you as a voice of reason and wisdom or do they hate to see you coming? Work on that.

17 PRODUCTIVELY BUSY

Proverbs 31:27- "She looketh well to the ways of her household, and eateth not the bread of idleness."

A virtuous business woman does not sit back and watch everyone else do what needs to be done! She is not annoyed when she is asked to help get something done. She understands that her reputation is at stake and that people talk. She knows how important it is for people to be able to put a face to the name.

When it comes to her home life, she is busy when she is at home. She is checking to make sure that her husband and children have everything that they need. She is doing whatever needs to be done in order for her home to run smoothly. She sits down and talks to her family. She prays with and for them. She makes sure that her relationships are solid!

A virtuous business woman checks to make sure that she and everyone else around her has what they need to get the job done. She accepts the blame when this does not happen. She does not try to put it on anyone else, even if she gave someone else the responsibility. She knows that anything that happens in her business is a direct reflection of her. She makes sure that, once her team comes in, they can get right to work and the project can be finished on time. She makes sure that no one is scrambling around trying to find supplies or figure out what to do.

A virtuous business woman steps in to help when and where she is needed. She does not carry herself as though she is too good to work. She does not tell people that she pays them to do those things. She may be busy at the time, but she finds a way to be involved in both situations. She may wear herself thin, but she rests in the fact that her team knows that they can count on her to not just be another pretty face. She wants to be known as someone who is willing to work!

A virtuous business woman is always busy doing something pertaining to the business. Some may say that she is not doing anything, but others trust that she is much busier than what she appears to be. She might be in front of three computer screens and on the phone at the same time, but the results are soon clear. She may not be in the office all day every day, but the reason is soon revealed. She may always been seen on TV or heard on the radio, but it is all about the business and how she can help it to grow. She may be in meetings from sunup to sundown, but that means that important business decisions are being made and vital partnerships are being formed. She may be sending a million emails, but it could result in everyone being helped and/or in the business making more money! She may never sit down and it may be because, if she does, something will not get done.

A virtuous business woman checks on her employees' personal and professional well-being. She takes time out of her day to sit and talk to each person that works for her. I remember when a former boss of mine did this. She met with everyone and asked them to bring in a copy of their resume. She wanted to make sure that people were in the best positions for them. She even asked them if they needed a raise, listened to why, and actually gave it to them! She moved many people around and we saw some leave, but we soon saw things working more cohesively because of what she did. She was helping people get to where they needed to be and where they could thrive! That is what a virtuous business woman does.

A virtuous business woman pays attention to everything and responds promptly. She does not sit back and wait to see if things are going to blow up before she says or does anything. She gets up and keeps that from happening. If she sees trouble coming, she is there standing in front of it. She solves what appears to be a problem before it becomes one. She does not wait for things to go wrong. She is so vigilant that sometimes she scares people, which is not a bad thing because that means they know that they need to be about business at all times. Her employees know that she is watching and knows everything that goes on. Think about a time when you have done something that you thought your boss did not see—only to end up in their office talking about that very issue!

Lastly, a virtuous business woman does not delegate for the purpose of sitting back with her feet up. She delegates because she needs help, to give others an opportunity to shine and show what they can do, to keep from snapping or breaking down, and to keep from quitting.

How are you using this verse? Are you using this verse? It is time to reflect on that now.

18 CROWN OF HER FAMILY

Proverbs 31:28- "Her children arise up, and call her blessed; her husband also, and he praiseth her."

A virtuous business woman has the love and support of her family! They are her first line of defense and the foundation of her support system. She works with them in mind and understands that everything that she says, does, and thinks affects them. She is careful not to get so bogged down with business that they are left stranded. They are her biggest cheerleaders!

A virtuous business woman is an example to her children. She behaves and carries herself in the way that she expects her children to. She does not do things in front of them for show—they can see through that! She shows them the value in hard work, how to properly spend money, and the importance of balance. Most importantly, she shows them a genuine walk and relationship with the Lord—they see Him working in their home and in her business. She leads by example.

I will never forget what happened when I allowed myself to start writing again. My daughter was extremely happy for me. As I sat there comparing prices from publishers, I noticed how much she was paying attention to what I was doing, so I started thinking out loud. She told me she wanted to use the same company for her own creations and, when I asked why, her reasons were more substantial than "Because you do." She watched and learned from me.

A virtuous business woman instills a sense of entrepreneurship in her children. She recognizes their gifts and talents early and cultivates them. She teaches them business principles on their level. She involves them in what she is doing. She finds ways for them to use their gifts and talents. She helps them to start their own businesses, even at a young age. She uses what she has learned to help them to grow and expand their thinking. She looks for a place in her business for what they have created. She channels their educational path based on their goals, which is not always easy to do. She helps them to read and research what it takes for them to do what they want to do. More importantly, she helps them to seek God's will for their lives in using those gifts and talents.

A virtuous business woman, again, has a business that utilizes the gifts and talents that her family possesses. Why do I keep talking about this? It is because this is something that I really want you to take the time to consider. You could be missing the person that could do better work than who you are about to pay. You may be about to endure a lot of frustration that could be avoided simply by letting your family help you. Do not sleep on the gifts and talents that are present in your family. Unearth them and put them to use!

A virtuous woman conducts herself in a manner that makes her family look good. In other words, no one is going to come back to her husband talking about what they saw her doing. She operates with thoughts of how her family would feel if they found out she didn't do things in the best way. She never does anything that would embarrass her husband. Her husband is able to defend her personal and professional actions without being laughed at because of something that everyone knows except him. This goes back to when we talked about her husband being able to trust her. She has to be careful of what she does both in public and in private.

Lastly, and again, a virtuous business woman's family knows that they come first. They know that they are important to her. She includes them. She cares for them. She shows that they matter. She is not working during family time. She calls home frequently when she is away. She is present in her child's school and at school events. It has to be a matter of national security for her to miss anything going on in her family life. She has balance.

I was reading the Facebook post once where a lady stated that her daughter caught her by the arm and told her that she missed her. She asked her what she was talking about and her daughter's response brought her to tears. Her daughter told her that she missed them spending time together. The mother did not understand what she meant. She worked from home and her child was homeschooled, so they were together all day every day. That was not what her daughter meant. They were not talking to each other unless she needed help with schoolwork. They were not eating meals together as much and, when they were, she only talked about business. She missed her mom!

For this chapter's exercise, I want you to evaluate yourself. What can you do to make sure that your family is taken care of and is not missing you?

19 NO LESS THAN EXCELLENCE

Proverbs 31:29-"Many daughters have done virtuously, but thou excellest them all."

A virtuous business woman strives for excellence! She does not take her position in her home nor in the world lightly. She understands how important it is do things in the best way. She understands that she has to give everything her best effort. She does not cut corners. She is not extremely cheap, yet she does not overspend. She understands the power of customer reviews. She strives to make sure that she gives the services and provides the products that she would want to receive. She wants people to recommend her!

A virtuous business woman is cognizant of others who have paved the way for her and builds on the legacies they set. She understands that she is where she is because of the efforts of other people.

Although she has broken through some barriers in her entrepreneurial journey, she knows that there are other women who fought and clawed for that to happen. She knows the history of the industrious women of the Bible and of those in world history. She sets out to leave a legacy that others behind her will want to follow themselves. She realizes that people are looking to her to set the standard and she sets it high, yet not so high that it can never be met.

A virtuous business woman, as we just said, realizes how important it is to be an example and to inspire others! She builds a business that is unique, yet somewhat easy to replicate. She uses what she learns to help others. She does not see those who want to learn as competition. She realizes that this person may be able to help someone that she may not be able to reach in her business. She establishes a support network and seeks to help other women who want to take that first crucial entrepreneurial step. She is raw, honest, and real in her counsel. She helps them to understand their value in the sight of God and others. She helps them to establish businesses that generate revenue and lead to goals being met. She reproduces herself as many times as she can before her time is done!

A virtuous business woman gives her best, does her best, works with the best, and produces the best. Let us talk about each one of those in detail. First, she gives her best—she is not haphazard or lazy in her dealings. She doesn't simply do what it takes to get by. She is not one that pacifies her clients; she genuinely serves them. She does not throw something together and expect for them to be okay with it simply because of who she is.

Next, she does her best—not the same as giving her best. When she does her best, she does not find herself wishing that she had done more or done better. She is not sitting back and hoping that they are not negatively impacted by her lack of effort.

She uses the best of materials in putting things together because she would want things to be done that way for her. She uses her ace materials and resources when called upon to help.

Then, she works with the best. While she tries to help those who are getting their businesses off the ground, she knows that quality comes with having a good track record. She is willing to invest a little more in working with someone who produces the results that she is looking for. She does her research on people and makes sure that they are a good fit for her business and the project at hand.

Last, she produces the best! She, again, creates what she would want to receive. She charges a price that she would be willing to pay if the situation were reversed, yet she does not just give her products away. She creates something of value that has a high demand. She revamps and refines what she already has out there when needed. She is always learning and looking for better ways to produce things. She is always in somebody's workshop or webinar learning a new skill that will help push her business to greater heights. Remember what we said about striving for excellence? That is a big part of it.

For this chapter, I want you to think about excellence. I want you to look at what you have created and ask yourself if you did that with a sense of urgency and feeling of excellence. If not, think about what you need to revamp and tweak, even if it is already out there. People revise and revamp things all the time. There is nothing wrong with doing better once you learn better, so get after it!

20 GOD-FEARING BUSINESS WOMAN

Proverbs 31:30- "Favour is deceitful, and beauty is vain: but a woman that feareth the Lord, she shall be praised."

We are coming to the end of our time together. If I had to pick one thought that was the most important, it would be this one.

A virtuous business woman is known as a woman of faith! She shares her faith will all that she contact with—she lets them know that her business is built on her faith. When she is asked why she does things a certain way, she responds with what God's word says about the matter. She is not afraid to start a meeting with prayer. She communicates the value of having God in her life and her business. She will be shunned and ridiculed. She may lose clients and money. However, she knows that God will provide because she stood firm in her faith and trust in

Him!

A virtuous business woman keeps God at the forefront of her business. She does nothing without prayer. She looks for answers in God's word. Before she does anything, she thinks about whether or not God would be pleased with that she is about to do. She has reminders around her that help to keep her on God's track for her life and business. She is always before God for her family, business, employees, and clients.

A virtuous business woman seeks to honor the Lord in all that she does in her business. She does not do business with any and every one. She operates by her core convictions, even when it costs her. Her business is built and run on Biblical principles. She is not going to do anything in her business that is contrary to God's will or God's way. What God thinks of her business is important to her!

A virtuous business woman does not allow

business to get in the way of her relationship with the Lord. She is not going to schedule a meeting or business matter of any kind at a time when she would be in church. She is in church if she is traveling. She gets her quiet time in with God before she starts her day. God is her first choice and not her last resort. She does not enter into a business partnership that is scripturally wrong, no matter how much money she stands to make from it!

A virtuous business woman PRAYS! She begins and ends her day with prayer. She is annoying to people at times because she tells them that she has to pray before she can give them an answer. Her business and family are immersed in prayer daily. There is never a time when she will not pray about a matter. She does not assume that anything is okay to do without praying first.

A virtuous business woman cares about how God feels and what His word says about a given issue.

She may read everything she gets her hands on in order to find a solution to her problem—and she may find one—yet, she will still pick up her Bible and ask God to show her how to deal with the situation in light of scripture. She understands the importance of consulting God and His word in both major and minor decisions. She, again, wants to do things in a way that is right and pleasing to God. She wants Him to be pleased in all that she endeavors and desires to do. She does not take Him, His word, nor His wisdom for granted.

Lastly, a virtuous business woman understands that good stewardship is a part of business and that God will hold her accountable for it. She realizes that she will have to answer both on earth and in Heaven for every decision she has made in her business. This drives her to make sure that she does both what is right and what is best in the eyes of God. She is not wasteful, slothful, or lazy; nor is she sneaky, conniving, or underhanded. She is not disrespectful nor rude and does things legally. She is a person of personal and professional integrity. She understands that the vision for her business came from God and He is entrusting her with it. She understands that she is His manager of what He has allowed her to build.

In the exercise for this chapter, I want you to think about God's place in your business. Does He have one? Are you known as a woman of faith? If not, how can you make that happen? If you are, how are you using that every day? Are you operating in light of the vision that God has for you or are you looking at it and doing things the way you want to do them? Think about it!

21 JUST SMILE AND WAVE

Proverbs 31:31-"Give her of the fruit of her hands; and let her own works praise her in the gates."

A virtuous business woman lets her work speak for her. She also speaks highly of what she does, yet without bragging or boasting. Huh? You can speak well of yourself without coming across as arrogant or cocky. There is a difference between that and confidence. Think about it!

A virtuous business woman has testimonials from those who have received her services. She can think that she is the best, yet her words are empty if she does not have any proof behind them. Her testimonials are not fabricated, either. She knows that what she is doing may be new. Even if she is her own first client, she has something to show for the work that she does.

A virtuous business woman produces goods and services that speak for themselves. Sometimes, she will not have to do any talking at all. When people look at her offerings, they know exactly what they are getting and she will be standing there smiling. They ask and answer their own questions, simply by looking at what she has put together for them.

A virtuous business woman has a benefit statement that entails what you can expect to receive from her company. You will know why she is the right person for the job. People will understand exactly what she is trying to do for them. They see the benefit in working with her. When they are cycling through comparisons in their minds, her company will still come to the forefront of their thoughts! She draws them in without saying a word!

Lastly, a virtuous business woman pays herself well without putting her business in jeopardy! How many times have you heard about companies going bankrupt because the owner could not get a handle on their personal spending with business funds? Exactly! A virtuous business woman would rather not take a salary from her business rather than destroy it. She creates multiple income streams and protects her business income in case of emergencies. She has a contingency plan for herself if she cannot take a salary from the business.

This last chapter is short because, as fun as this has been, it is the end of our journey through Proverbs 31. For this chapter's exercise, I really want you to think about whether or not you are doing this and what you need to do for this to happen. It is time to pray, ponder, and plan!

It is my hope and prayer that this journey has been beneficial for you. We have talked about many things that many women do not think about and are not willing to do. I wish you God's best in all that you do and create!

A WORD FROM THE AUTHOR

A million thank yous to you for diving into the second edition of The Virtuous Business Woman: Inspired by Proverbs 31! Usually, I would've said this in the beginning, but I decided to wait until you finished.

I created the second edition after numerous people said that they wished the book was separated and, after creating a separate book and workbook combo for my Slayers project, I realized that this really did need to be done and was quite possible to do!

I wanted the women reading this book to be able to dissect it the way that she needed to without the worksheets causing her to pause her reading before she was ready to. That's another piece of feedback I received and was reminded of while formatting the book into a smaller size.

I also thought about the women who wanted to pass the book along without people seeing her inner thoughts and struggles! The worksheet PDF was good, but I believe this is better.

So if you wanted to know why I did this, the answer is simple,
I did it for you!

If you are reading this page and you feel like you need a shoulder to lean on, a helping hand, a sounding board, or a kick…or nudge…or punch in the right direction, I am here for you! My goal is to help you to Rise above your frustration, Reclaim your life and talents, and Evolve into the woman who is free to transform those talents into a treasure—a God-honoring business, all while maintaining a strong family base. We can work through this book together and help you to be the Virtuous Business Woman both you and God want you to be!

If you are ready, all it takes is an email to mompreneurengineer@gmail.com. You may be in Phoenix Mode now, but you're not meant to stay there…

Talk to you soon!

Tammie

www.ingramcontent.com/pod-product-compliance
Lightning Source LLC
Chambersburg PA
CBHW071439180526
45170CB00001B/382